Questions and Feelings About . . .

Worries

by Paul Christelis

illustrated by Ximena Jeria

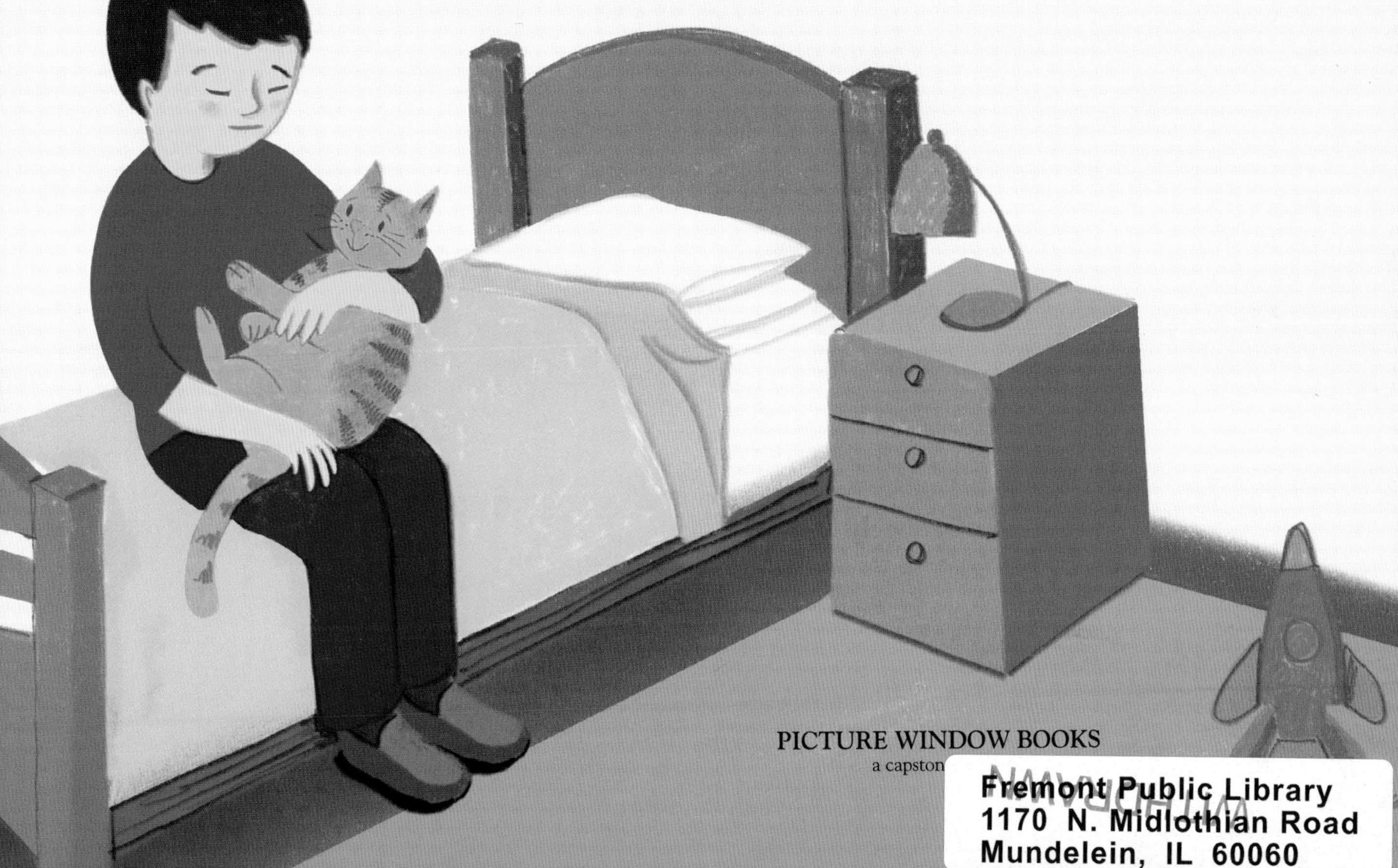

PICTURE WINDOW BOOKS
a capston

Questions and Feelings About . . . is published by
Picture Window Books, a Capstone imprint
1710 Roe Crest Drive, North Mankato, MN 56003
www.mycapstone.com

Library of Congress Cataloging-in-Publication Data is available on the Library of Congress website.

ISBN: 978-1-5158-4544-7 (library binding)

Editor: Melanie Palmer
Design: Lisa Peacock
Author: Paul Christelis

First published in Great Britain in 2018
by The Watts Publishing Group

Printed and bound in China.
001593

Questions and Feelings About . . .

Worries

Have you ever worried about something? Maybe you've been invited to a party and you're worried that you won't know anyone else. Or perhaps someone you love is ill and you're concerned about what might happen to them.

We all have worries from time to time.
Parents, friends, and teachers can all worry.
It's a normal part of life.

What do you worry about?

When worries fill our heads, they can make us feel anxious. Anxiety can make us feel unwell.

We might feel all wobbly inside,
or our hearts might beat faster.
Maybe our bellies ache, or
we don't feel like eating.

How do you feel when you are worried?

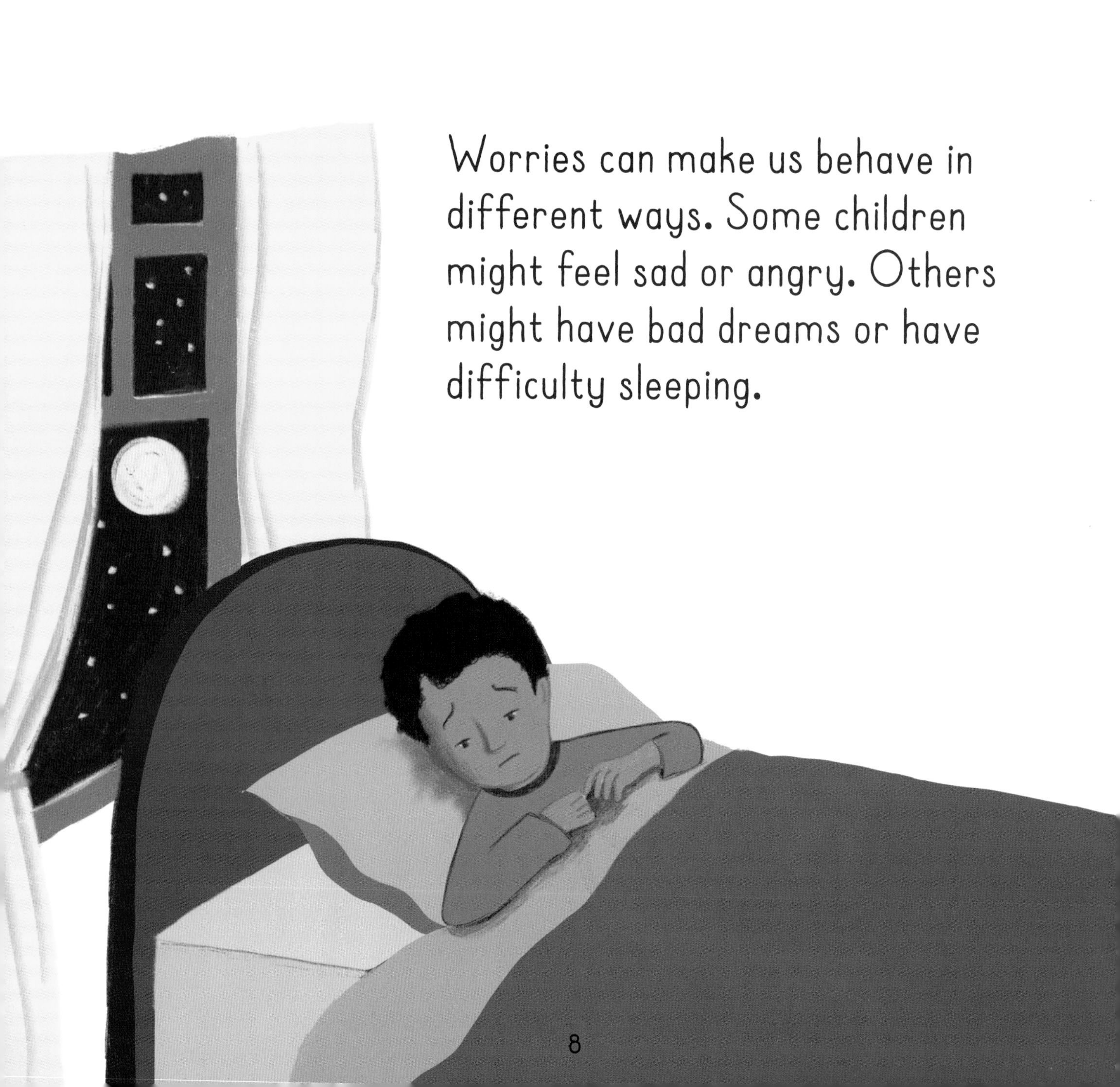

Worries can make us behave in different ways. Some children might feel sad or angry. Others might have bad dreams or have difficulty sleeping.

You might find it difficult to concentrate or feel scared to try new things. Or you might not feel like going to school or spending time away from your loved ones.

Sometimes worrying can be useful because it tells us that something is wrong and that we need to get help. If your friend got hurt at the playground, you would worry for them and take them to the school nurse or call a teacher.

But worrying can also be unhelpful. This happens when we imagine bad things happening to us even though there is nothing wrong.

Sometimes we may worry about bad things happening by asking ourselves "What if" questions, such as "what if I fell out of a tree?" or "what if my dog was ill?"

What questions would you ask yourself?

Worries are nothing more than unfriendly thoughts. The more we think them, the more anxious they can make us feel.

But there is good news! Even though these thoughts feel real, they are not.

They are only thoughts. You can't hold a thought in your hand or see the shape of a thought.

Try it for yourself. Think about a pink elephant. Can you see one in your mind? That pink elephant is only a thought. You can't really touch it or smell it, can you?

It’s the same with worries. Even though the worries are not real things, our bodies still feel anxious when we think them. Our bodies believe that the worries are real!

What can you do to make yourself feel better when you are worrying? Luckily, there are many things that can help.

You can choose to place your attention on something that is happening now rather than get lost in worries about the future. A good place to start is to focus on your breathing.

See if you can feel the air moving into your nose as you breath in and out of your nose as you breath out. Notice how each breath is different.

You can also notice what's going on around you. If you are outdoors, you might feel the warm sun on your skin or see the colors and shapes of plants and trees.

Listening to sounds can be very calming. Birds tweeting. A breeze blowing. Music playing. See how many different sounds you can notice.

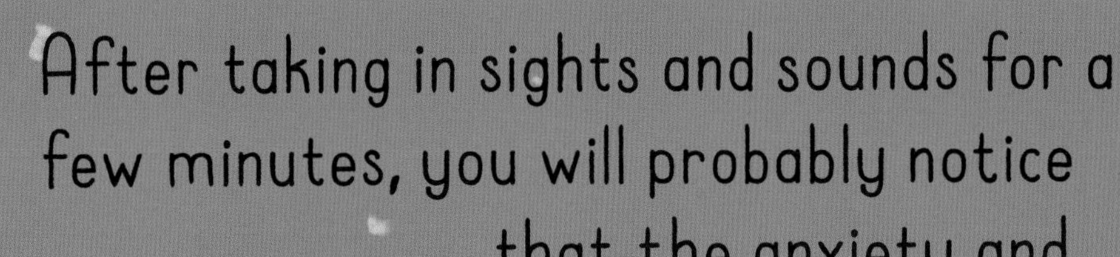

After taking in sights and sounds for a few minutes, you will probably notice that the anxiety and the worries are not so loud anymore.

What do you hear when you are outside?

It also helps to write your worries down or draw them. Once you have done this, fold up the paper and place it in a Worry Box (you could use a shoe box or tissue box).

Place the Worry Box on a shelf or in a drawer. You can open the box at the end of the week and empty the worries. You might realize that they aren't worries anymore.

Sometimes all we need to do when we are feeling worried about something is to talk to someone. It could be our parents, caregivers, brothers, sisters, friends, or anyone we trust. Even our pets!

Sharing our worries helps us move the anxious feelings out of our bodies. It's like opening a window in a stuffy room. Fresh air flows in and everyone feels better.

It's also helpful to remember that very often things seem worse in our imaginations than they really are . . .

. . . and we are often a lot braver and more able than we think!

Notes for Caregivers

As a parent, teacher, or guardian, the most important thing you can offer a worrying child is your time and attention. Listen to their concerns. Let them know that it's normal to have worries. Everyone experiences these at times. Once you have provided a safe and non-judgemental space for the child to express his or her concerns, there are effective ways to help soothe them. Here are a few suggestions:

Let your child know that the worrying thoughts are simply thoughts. They are like traffic. Cars come and go all day. Sometimes there are many and sometimes not. It can be unpleasant to be stuck in traffic, but sooner or later the road will clear and the noise of the traffic will fade. Worries are similar. Thinking about them can be noisy and unpleasant, but if we are patient we notice that they don't last.

Worrying thoughts usually show up in the body as unpleasant sensations. Identifying and naming these sensations in a calm and kind manner is a powerful way of helping your child deal with the unpleasantness without amplifying the worry. Diverting attention from the worry to the sensation of breathing can calm the anxiety associated with worrying. It's easy to do and only takes a few moments.

Having enough sleep, a healthy, balanced daily diet, and regular exercise will promote physical and mental well-being and help equip children better manage worry and anxiety.

Group Activities

1. Discuss how worries can be dealt with by making a Worry Box (like on pages 24–25). Ask children to write their worries down and put them in the box. At the end of the day (or week), they can throw their worries away.

2. Ask children to write down any unpleasant sensations they feel when they worry. Then ask them to pair up and share what they wrote. How do they feel the same as their partner? How do they feel different? This activity will show them that everyone worries.

3. One effective breath exercise for keeping calm is 7–11 breathing. Breathe in through the nose to the count of 7, pause, and then breathe out through the nose to the count of 11 (repeat this a few times). This enables the out breath to be longer than the in breath. This allows the parasympathetic nervous system (PSN) to become activated and sooth the stress response in the body.

Read More:

Green, Andi. *Don't Feed the Worry Bug*. Monsters in My Head Publishing, 2011.

Merritt, Susanne. *Don't Think About Purple Elephants*. EK Books, 2015.

Thomas, Isabel. *Dealing with Feeling Worried*. Heinemann, 2013.

Read the entire Questions and Feelings About . . . series:

Adoption
Autism
Bullying
Having a Disability
Racism
When Parents Separate
When Someone Dies
Worries